P9-CSG-497

No Bored Babies

A Guide to making Developmental Toys
For babies birth to age two

by
Jan Fisher Shea

Bear Creek Publications
Seattle, Washington

Copyright © 1986 Bear Creek Publications
All rights reserved. Printed in the United States of
America.

No part of this book may be used or reproduced in any
manner whatsoever without written permission except
in the case of brief quotations embodied in critical
articles and reviews. For information address:

Bear Creek Publications
2507 Minor Ave E.
Seattle, Washington 98102

Second Edition
    First Printing-December, 1986
    Second Printing-March, 1987
    Third Printing-May, 1989
    Fourth Printing-May, 1990
    Fifth Printing-April, 1991

Book Design by Barbara Beach Moody, The Laser's Edge
Photographs by Anita Coolidge
Cover Design and illustrations on pages 12, 20, 21, 24,
26, 31, 32, 33, 34, 35, 36, 38, 41, 43, 45, 49, 50, 56,
and 58, by Jeanne Edwards

Library of Congress Cataloging-in-Publication Data
Shea, Jan Fisher, 1951-

    No Bored Babies.

    Bibliography: p.

1. Toy making. 2. Educational toys. 3. Child
Development. I.Title. TT174.S48 1986 745.592
85-30783
ISBN 0-936005-02-5(pbk.)

Distributed by Gryphon House, Inc.
P.O. Box 275
Mt. Rainier, MD 20712

Dedication

To all those parents who spent hundreds of dollars on toys, only to watch their child play with the boxes.
Let's get even.

For Dan & Heather —
Hope you have fun
with your new baby!
With Love,
Margaret, Steve,
and Ricky
Lindsey

A Note from the Author

Like many mothers, I wanted to provide my child with a stimulating environment. I trusted the toys I had received as shower gifts would do this. But it didn't take me long to figure out that my son didn't find his toys as entertaining as adults did.

I started reading books on childhood development. From these books, I figured out simple things I could put together.

My son responded. I could tell he related to the Raggedy Ann face on the soft blocks I had made. He would grab the block and stare at the face — such a different response from letting the pale yellow rattle fall from his hand every time I placed it there.

There are many "growth toys" on the market. They are for the most part expensive, designed for adults, and quickly "out grown."

This book is designed to help you make things at home to develop your child's cognitive, physical, sensory and perceptual skills during the first two years of life. The ideas are easy and simple and may serve to help you develop some of your own designs. I hope you and your baby have a fun and productive time.

Jan Fisher Shea

P.S. The words "he" and "his" have been used throughout the book simply because I've patterned the book around my son. Of course all the information presented applies to both sexes.

Table of Contents

Why Make Your Own Toys..7

Setting Up Your Toy Workshop...8

Safety..11

The Visual Crib..13
The Newborn - Birth To 6 Weeks

Batting Practice Time...21
6 Weeks - 3 Months

Reaching, Grasping, Chewing and Kicking........................27
3 Months to 6 Months

The Mover and Shaker..33
6 to 9 Months

The Explorer...39
9 to 14 Months

Challenge...49
14 to 24 Months

Household Objects as Toys..61

Thanks to:
The staff at Evergreen and Overlake Hospitals, Northwest Baby, the Secret Garden Children's Bookshop and the Seattle Children's Museum for their cooperation and enthusiasm.

Frank and Kevin for their patience, support and enthusiasm for all my crazy ideas.

My co-conspirator Kathy for the inspiration, wisdom and hard work.

And special thanks to the following babies and their parents; Steven Reed, Daniel Cutler, Nicholas and Benjamin Merth, Rashawn Moses, and cover girls Alison Louise Fisher and Laura Marie Shea.

WHY MAKE YOUR OWN TOYS

Toys are not just a means of entertainment for babies, but tools to learn about their world. In the first two years of life there is a lot to learn, so babies invent toys all the time. It may look like a wooden spoon, a telephone cord, or junk mail to you, but to a baby, it's a toy.

Many of the toys on the market are created with more attention to commercial success than play value. That's why many babies abandon toys in favor of the box or the paper bag they came in.

This book is designed to help you get to know your baby and his changing needs. The toys in *No Bored Babies* are made from everyday objects--milk cartons, boxes, coffee cans, egg cartons, thread spools, coat hangers--and the list goes on. The toys are easy to construct and take only a short time to assemble.

Remember, your baby doesn't care how much his toys cost. He's too busy discovering the world for the first time and just wants lots of new experiences.

SETTING UP YOUR TOY WORKSHOP

As you go through this book you will find lots of everyday things that can be used to make toys. I suggest you have a box hidden in a closet somewhere to store these things until the time is right to use them.

The following is a list of things to start collecting:

Household items

Tennis balls
Cylindrical oatmeal and salt boxes
Shoe boxes
Styrofoam meat trays
Gift boxes
Egg cartons
Cardboard cartons
Band aid boxes
Greeting cards
Milk cartons
Old magazines
Shirt and pantyhose cardboard
Cardboard tubes
Paper plates
Pie tins
Plastic shampoo, detergent and bleach bottles
Film canisters
Plastic 2 liter pop containers
Colored sponges
Fabric swatches
Coat hangers
Gloves
Tin cans
Wooden and plastic spoons
Scarves

The following is a list of **tools** to collect for your workshop. Many you probably have around the house.

Scissors
Sandpaper
Ruler
Exacto Knife
Knitting needle
Steel wool
Paint brush
Needle
Paper punch

The following items may need **to be purchased**, but then I'm always surprised to find how many people have these things just laying around the house.

Poster board
Colored construction paper
Con-Tact paper--clear, colored and patterned
Felt
Polyester fiberfill
Elastic
Velcro
Ribbons
Buttons
Thread
Ping pong balls
Balloons
Cloth or plastic tape
Felt tip markers
Non-toxic paint
Light and heavy weight string
Yarn
Non-toxic glue
Epoxy cement

SAFETY

Just a few words about safety before we get to the meat of this book. Most articles and chapters on safety are filled with "don't lists." Since this is an action book I don't want to slow you down by telling you everything you should not do.

Throughout the book there are warnings about certain toys. Please pay special attention to this symbol for these warnings.

 **SAFETY NOTE**

Child safety revolves around five basic rules.

1. Stay tuned to your baby's changing abilities and select toys that are appropriate to his age and stage of development.

If your baby is sprouting teeth, he will do well with a teething toy, but not with one that is stuffed with beans where he could bite a hole. If your child is attempting to crawl, a rolling toy will be just the thing, but you'd better take down the fragile mobile over his crib as soon as he starts reaching and grasping.

2. To a baby everything is a toy. Anything a baby can touch is fair game to him. A comb, your favorite piece of crystal, the cat--they are all toys.

3. Babies will put all toys in their mouths. Wash all materials and containers before using. Use only paints, markers, glues and adhesives labeled non-toxic. Make sure all objects are larger than 1" x 2".

4. Rough edges scratch and cut; pointed edges poke. Corners should be rounded or cushioned with tape. Sand surfaces that may splinter.

5. Check out every "toy" yourself before you give it to your child. That goes for store bought presents to gifts grandma makes. When constructing toys, use extra care to make them properly, even if it takes a little extra time. Care should be used to position any hanging toys or mobiles so they are secure.

The toys described in this book are designed to be safe. Toys, however, should be checked from time to time for breakage and to make sure the glue, tape, or epoxy is still holding it together.

The most important rule of all with children's toys is to use your common sense.

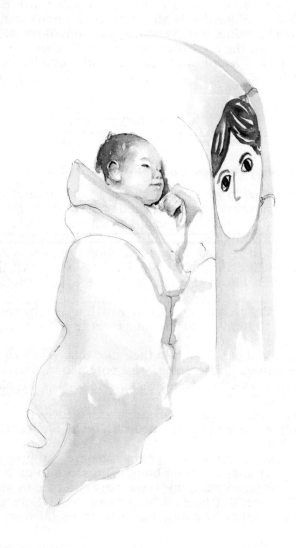

THE VISUAL CRIB
The Newborn--Birth to 6 weeks

To better understand your newborn, let's look at what the latest research has to say about them. They are attracted to sharp, contrasting colors such as black and white, and bold patterns such as checkerboards, diagonals, and bull's-eyes. A young baby's favorite pattern is a simple picture of the human face. Research also shows that newborns look to the far right 90% of the time and the far left the remaining 10%. They best see in the 7-9 inch range.

With appropriately designed pictures and mobiles you can help your baby "learn by looking." Granted, your baby's alert moments will be brief in the first month, but in providing things he likes to look at, you'll be giving him the opportunity to exercise his visual abilities.

The following ideas will help you create "toys" known to appeal to very young babies.

Art Museum

By taping pictures to the side of a crib or bassinet, baby can have his own "art museum." Draw black and white diagonals, bull's-eyes, and checkers on 5 inch by 5 inch white poster board. Stickers of panda bears, zebras, and giraffes can make a stimulating yet decorative lining to baby's bassinet or cradle.

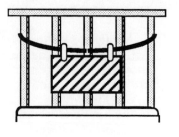

To help baby continue to "discover" his world, replace one picture or pattern every couple of days.

A simple drawing of the human face emphasizing the eyes, nose, and hair can keep baby entertained for months. Draw the face on a 6" by 7" piece of poster board and cut out the face to give it more definition. Place the face drawing in baby's art museum.

Inside of Bassinet

Later, you can tape this picture so baby can see it while riding in the car. (Don't be surprised if you see your 2 month old baby smiling and "talking" to this picture.)

VIsual Mobiles

Another way to help your baby develop his visual skills is with mobiles. The patterns and bright colors combined with movement will attract baby's attention to the object, encouraging focusing and eye movement.

The following ideas can save you a condsiderable amount of money over store bought mobiles (can you believe the prices on those things!), while allowing you the option to make endless variations.

Here are a few hints for successful mobile crafting.
- Use 3-4 objects
- Replace 1 object every few days
- Consider the baby's view of the objects
- Make sure all objects are light weight and securely fastened
- Use bright colors or patterns with sharp, contrasting colors
- Position mobile 7 - 9 inches from baby's eyes
- Position mobile to either right or left side (not in the middle)

There are several ways to construct mobiles from household objects depending on what you have on hand.

Things to Hang

The graphic designs used to create the art museum can be incorporated into a mobile--just make sure the patterns face down so baby can see them. Try out these patterns in 3-D. Toilet paper rolls, cereal boxes, and jar lids can be used to add dimension to your designs.

Try hanging the following items. Use your resources and imagination for variation.

- Curtain rings
- Plastic fruit
- Thread spools
- Seed Packets
- Feathers
- Key rings
- Playing cards
- Rubber gloves
- Cereal Boxes
- Foil pans
- Cardboard shapes
- Plastic measuring spoons or cups
- Pictures or photographs mounted on cardboard
- Wooden utensils
- Yarn fuzz balls
- Sponges or pot scrubbers
- Costume jewelry
- Styrofoam balls
- Tiny stuffed animals
- Decorated paper plates

Mounting the Mobile

After constructing your mobiles, you will need a way to suspend them within your baby's focusing range. Here are just a few ideas. Take a little extra time to see that they are securely mounted.

- Plant hangers
- Cabinet handle
- Ceiling hook
- Chair
- Coat hanger molded into circle or square shape and mounted to wall with push pin or nail.

SAFETY NOTE

Remove molded coat hangers when baby starts to reach and grab.

Pie Tin Mobile

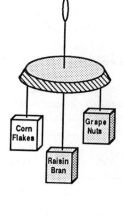

Aluminum pie plate
Yarn, string, fishing line etc.
Assorted household objects

1. Punch hole through middle
of pie tin.
2. Punch 3 - 4 evenly spaced holes
through rim of pie tin.
3. Thread string, yarn, or fishing
line through the holes and knot securely.
4. Hang object from string attached to rim (balance them as
you go).
5. Make loop at top of string threaded through middle of pie
tin and hang.

Coat Hanger Mobile

It's best to use a hanger with a cardboard roll, like the kind
used for hanging pants. If you don't have one, an ordinary
hanger will work.

Coat hanger
Light weight string or yarn
Assorted household objects

1. Cut 1 ft lengths of string.
2. Cut grooves in cardboard roll
and tie string.
3. Attach objects so they hang 7 - 9
inches from baby's eyes.

For added color, cover cardboard roll with cloth tape or paint
with non-toxic paint.

Embroidery Hoop Mobile

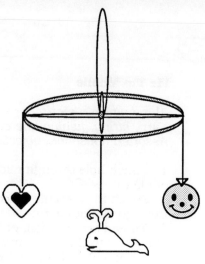

Embroidery hoop
(or other type of ring)
Heavy weight string or yarn
Assorted household objects

1. Tie two lengths of string to
embroidery hoop so that it makes
a cross in middle of hoop.
2. Tie another piece of string where
cross pieces of string meet and form
loop for hanging.
3. Attach objects to hoop with string.
Slide stringed objects around on hoop
until they balance.
4 . Double knot objects in place when balanced.

Colored Jars

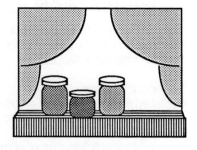

Several small jars with lids
Assorted food coloring
water

1. Fill jars with water.
2. Add a few drops of food
coloring to each jar.
3. Stack or arrange jars near
sunny window next to baby's crib.

This will create beautiful patterns of light coming into baby's
room.

Reflection Mobile

Basic mobile support
Cardboard
Aluminum Foil and glue
or silver contact paper

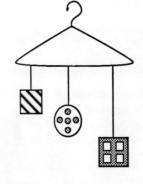

1. Cut cardboard into patterns or various 3 dimensional shapes.
2. Decorate with foil or contact paper.
3. Attach to pie tin, coat hanger or embroidery hoop mobile
4. Place in front of window to catch interesting patterns of light. Try the illustrated designs or create some of your own.

Other Ideas

An ordinary ceiling hook can hold a variety of household items such as scarves, ribbons, Christmas decorations, or balloons. You may want to position the ceiling hook directly over baby's crib and move the crib so the objects hang to the right of baby. Hang near open window, air current, or fan. Attach these items to long strings or strings on coat hangers to position them within your baby's focusing range. At about age 2 months baby should have the head control to look straight ahead. This is when the crib can be realigned.

These few simple hints will give baby a visually enriched environment. When baby makes attempts to grab at his "art museum" it is time to rearrange--he can focus better and wants to touch.

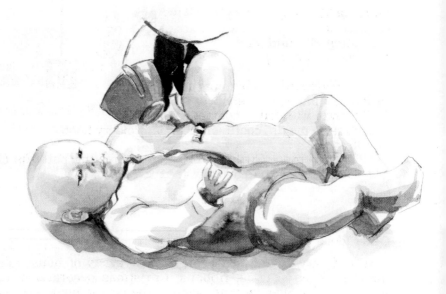

BATTING PRACTICE TIME
6 weeks - 3 months

At this stage your baby starts to look straight ahead. His hands open up. He wants to feel surfaces. He swipes and kicks at objects then tries to bring them to his mouth.

As your baby reaches out to touch things, it is time to move his fragile mobiles a yard away and replace them with safe, hanging "batting" toys.

Three types of toys work well for baby at this time--mobiles to look at, bat-mobiles to swipe at, and feelie toys to touch.

Mobiles

At this stage mobiles can be hung over the center of the crib. If you used the hook in the ceiling described in the last section, continue to exchange streamers, balloons, scarves, bright colored paper plates, or napkins.

Pictures of faces will still be a big hit with babies this age. They now pay attention to 3 dimensional forms that are more complete.

On a white paper plate, draw a happy face on one side and a sad face on the other. Or make a face with brightly colored yarn on a tin foil pie plate. Faces can be drawn on balloons. Face pictures from magazines can be mounted on cardboard.

Bat-Mobiles

Bat-mobiles should be hung from a dowel placed across baby's crib, playpen, or between two chairs while baby is lying on the floor. If you have an adjustable crib it is best to put the mattress in the lowest position. This will better facilitate hanging toys for batting and viewing.

Bat-Mobile Holder

Dowel
Eyelet screws and
heavyweight string **or**
Velcro and glue

1. Attach small eyelet screws or velcro to both the dowel and baby's crib or playpen.
2. Attach small eyelet screws to dowel to facilitate hanging toys.

SAFETY NOTE

Do not hang mobiles from anything that slings across baby's crib or playpen.

What You Should Hang

Any colorful, light weight household objects that **do not** have sharp edges can be used for "batting" practice. Suspend these "toys" from a dowel above baby's crib or playpen. The toys should be 6 - 8 inches from baby.

In addition to the items listed in the previous section, let the following ideas spark your imagination.

- Shiny plastic beach balls
- Plastic streamers
- "Wooly" ball
- Light weight rattles
- Rag dolls
- Chiming ball
- Decorated ping pong balls
- Plastic Easter eggs
- Decorated panty hose containers

Portable Bat Mobiles can be made using the **Coat Hanger Mobiles** described in the last section. These are great to take along to baby-sitters, grandma's or when setting up a play area for baby away from his normal haunts. Hangers that have a cardboard base work best.

Ping pong balls can be painted with black bull's-eyes, diagonals, check-erboards, sunbursts, and faces or covered with bright colored contact paper. Make two slits in the ping pong balls and slide knotted string through to secure to the hanger.

Cloth or contact covered egg-shaped panty hose containers or plastic Easter eggs make and attrac-tive portable bat-mobile. These containers can be filled with dried beans or buttons to lend sound to the batting experience.

SAFETY NOTE

Eggs filled with beans or buttons should be glued shut with epoxy. Check eggs before each use to be sure glue has not loosened.

A **Stuffed Animal Bat Mobile** can be made from 4 or 5 small 6 - 8 " toy animals, a 8" metal ring or embroidery hoop, and either string or strong yarn. Hang the animals facing down towards the baby.

With batting toys, remember to hang things near baby's hands. When he becomes bored, move them towards his feet so he can learn to kick.

Feelie Toys

Your baby also enjoys feeling surfaces with his hands during this time and this is where feelie toys come in.

Assorted fabrics
  ex: fake fur
        velvet
        burlap
        vinyl
        terry cloth
        brocade
        silky or slippery fabrics.
*Rounded wooden clothes pins (for **feelie sticks**)*
*Cardboard (for **feelie mural**)*
Glue

1. Make a **Feelie Blanket** for use in the crib, car seat, or stroller by sewing together swatches of 5 or 6 different fabrics each about 5" square.

24

2. Make **Feelie Sticks** by gluing fabrics to old fashioned (rounded) clothes pins.

3. Make a **Feelie Mural** by gluing fabric pieces on cardboard to create a collage of color and texture.

Hang on wall next to baby's changing table.

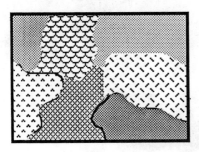

Smiling Sheet

Solid colored crib sheet
Dark colored fabric scrap

1. Create a smiling face with fabric scraps.
2. Sew to right side of crib sheet where it is visible to your baby.

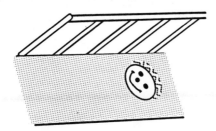

REACHING, GRASPING, CHEWING AND KICKING
3 to 6 Months

Your baby at this stage is on his way to becoming an intelligent human being. Many parents feel like they are now dealing with a "person."

During this phase he will aquire vision that is as good as an adult's and can engage in more focused eye-hand behavior. He is interested in exploring objects by grasping and chewing.

He will begin using both hands to pick up objects as well as transfer them from one hand to another.

Other new abilities include kicking and rolling over. Toys can be used to develop and work on these new skills.

If your baby spends a good part of his day having pleasant and exciting experiences, he will be better off than one who has to spend the day staring at the ceiling. You can very easily set up an environment for him to experience a lot of new things every day.

Once your child has entered the reaching and grasping stage, you should put away the batting toys. Objects that swing away when touched will be very frustrating to him.

SAFETY NOTE

All toys from this stage on should be safe enough to put in the mouth. This means no sharp edges, points, loose parts, or toxic finishes.

Chewable Books

Colorful magazine pictures
*Plastic photo album page **or***
Cardboard & clear contact paper
Glue

1. Cut album pages in half to make them more "baby size".
2. Glue the pictures onto the cardboard.
3. If not using photo album pages, cover with clear contact paper.

DISCOVERY TOYS

An **Unbreakable Mirror** which can be found in many stores that carry backpacking equipment provides a lot of entertainment for baby. Mount the mirror on a wall next to the changing table about seven inches away from baby's face.

Bracelets for fingers and toes can attract your baby's attention to his feet and hands if he has not yet noticed them. Attach a large bell to 1/4 inch elastic with a little overlap to fit toes. You can use a pair of brightly colored infant socks cut down to fit around fingers or wrists.

Embroider a face on one of your baby's socks to make a **Face Sock.** Have baby wear this to attract attention to his feet.

GRASPING TOYS

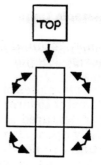

Soft Blocks

6 fabric squares
about 6 x 6 inches
Polyester stuffing **or**
Old nylons
Jingle bells and
plastic film canister (optional)

1. Sew fabric squares together to form cube leaving one seam open.
2. Stuff block with polyester stuffing or old nylons.
3. To give the block "sound" put jingle bells inside a plastic film canister and   place in center of block .
4. Sew up open seam by hand.

Use material with patterns like checks or polka dots. Fabrics that have faces like Raggedy Ann or Andy or patterns like bright flowers should be centered to make the most out of these pieces.

Variations of Soft Blocks

• Substitute textured fabrics like fur, burlap, terry cloth, oil cloth, velvet, or brocade.
• Applique letters, numbers, or dots (like dice) onto solid colored squares of block.

Squeezable Donut

Scraps of textured fabric
Polyester fiberfill

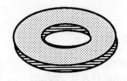

1. Cut two pieces of fabric 6 inches in diameter to form donut shape.
2. Put textured sides together and sew, leaving inner seam partially open. Turn.
3. Stuff with fiberfill and hand stitch closed.
The donut shape is particularly easy for babies to grab and pick up.

Dinner Bell

Empty tennis ball can with lid
Dried beans or bells
Epoxy cement
Con-Tact paper **or**
  fabric and glue
Wide ribbon
Curtain ring

1. Punch hole through bottom of can and lid.
2. Add beans or bells to can.
3. Thread ribbon through holes.
4. Seal lid with contact cement.
5. Cover can with Con-Tact paper or fabric.
6. Tie curtain ring to one end of ribbon.
7. Hang from crib dowel or baby carriage hood within baby's reach so he can make it ring.

KICKING TOYS

When making **Kicking Toys** , tie the ends of the string or elastic to the crib posts so the toy will lie 1 1/2 inches above the mattress. Show your baby how to kick the toy by guiding his feet through a couple of kicks. He'll take it from there.

Kicking Box

Oatmeal box
Heavy string
Noisemakers
  ex : dried beans
          buttons
          jingle bells
Glue
Cloth tape

1. Poke a hole in the bottom of the box and lid.
2. Thread a 5 foot section of string through the holes.
3. Add noisemakers and glue the lid on.
4. Tape seams.

Kicking Board

1/4 inch plywood or masonite
3/4 inch waist band elastic
Non-toxic paint

1. Cut a 13 x 15 inch rectangle out of wood.
2. Sand wood and paint colorful design.
3. Drill a hole in each corner.
4. Thread with 12 inch lengths of heavy 3/4 inch waist band elastic.
5. Secure elastic to crib bars about 6 inches from foot of bed.

Kicking Bottle

2 empty plastic 2 liter beverage containers
Epoxy contact cement
Plastic or cloth tape
Objects
  ex: bell
      toy animal
      ball
Heavy string

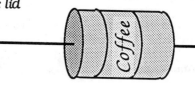

1. Cut top 1/3 off of bottle.
2. Poke hole through bottoms.
3. Thread string through holes and knot on inside.
4. Place objects inside.
5. Glue together with contact cement. Tape seam.
This toy should be able to spin when baby kicks it.

Kicking Can

Large coffee can with plastic lid
Dried beans or bells
Contact cement
Heavy weight string
*Con-Tact paper **or***
  fabric and glue

1. Punch holes in bottom and lid of coffee can.
2. Add beans and or bells.
3. Thread string through holes.
4. Seal lid with contact cement.
5. Decorate with Con-Tact paper or fabric.

This is another toy that should be able to spin when baby kicks it.

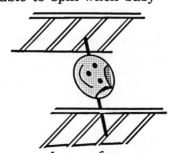

Kicking Pillow

Small pillow
3/4 inch waist band elastic
Fabric

1. Sew or embroider a colorful pattern such as a face or a bull's-eye in the pillow.
2. Sew two pieces of 3/4 inch waist band elastic to sides of pillow and attach elastic to crib sides.

THE MOVER AND SHAKER
6 to 9 Months

Experts claim that the foundations of intelligence are formed during this period of a baby's life. By staying aware of your child's abilities and interests you can elevate the quality of his daily experiences.

The concept of "object permanence" can be taught through peek-a-boo games with objects and you. Learning that people and objects continue to exist even when they are no longer in sight will boost his sense of trust in the world.

He needs to be able to play with some small objects and the opportunity to work simple mechanisms and solve very simple problems. He is exploring the cause and effect relationships his hands can have on objects—such as throwing a toy over the side of his crib or high chair. Baby watches the object fall and hears the sound it makes when it hits the floor. He will bang an object against a surface to hear the sound it will make.

Soon your baby will be able to sit on his own. His orientation to the world and playthings will change.

During these months he will also move about in his own fashion, whether it be scooting on his elbows or bottom, rocking back and forth on hands and knees or regular crawling.

Babies at this stage like to practice turning over, sitting alone, and exercising their arms and legs. They are interested in sound, especially in their parent's voices.

There are several household items that can be used to develop his new skills.

"CAUSE AND EFFECT" NOISEMAKES

These are toys that baby can bang around. Baby is actually making a noise. He is learning that his actions cause a sound.

Shaking and Banging Toy

Empty thread spools
Shoe string

1. Thread spools on shoe string.
2. Tie ends together.

Rattle Box

Clear plastic storage box with several compartments
Small noisemakers
  ex buttons
       popcorn
       beads
       sequins
Contact cement
Cloth tape

1. Place noisemakers in the different compartments of the storage box.
2. Glue lid to box with contact cement.
3. After glue has dried, seal seam with cloth tape.

This is an excellent way for baby to get close to things he normally can't touch.

SAFETY NOTE

Check *Rattle Box*   before each use for cracking of box or loosening of tape.

Drum

Oatmeal box **or**
  coffee can
Tape
Plastic, wooden or metal spoons
Con-Tact paper **or**
  fabric and glue.

1. Pound down edges of coffee can and tape open ends of oatmeal box or coffee can.
2. Replace lid and glue in place.
3. Decorate outside of can with Con-Tact paper or fabric and glue.

Let him use plastic, wooden or metal spoons to vary the sound.

Shaker Rattle

2 aerosol can lids
Contact cement
Cloth adhesive tape
Noisemakers
  ex : dried beans
      peas
      popcorn
      buttons
      bells

1. Put beans or other noisemakers in one lid.
2. Glue second lid in place over filled lid.
3. After glue has dried , tape seam securely with tape.

Shaker Rattles can be used later to shake to music.

Pop Bottle Roller

Two empty 2 liter
  beverage containers
Small toys
Epoxy cement
Cloth or plastic tape

1. Cut top 1/3 off of each beverage container.
2. Put toys inside bottom of 1 container.
3. Align second beverage container bottom so it forms one closed unit and glue with contact cement.
4. Tape seam with cloth or plastic tape.

This will make a good moving toy for the baby learning to crawl.

High Chair Toy Retrieval

3 pieces of 2 foot string
Different weighted objects
  ex: feather
      balloon
      ping-pong ball

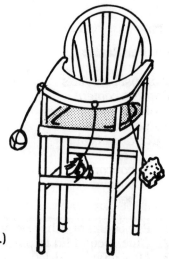

1. Attach objects to string with glue or by tying. (ex: slit ping-pong ball and slip knotted string through.)
2. Tie other end of string to baby's highchair.

Your baby can check the cause and effect of throwing these various objects.

Stroller or High Chair Toy Holder

Elastic, string, or shoe lace
Choices of:
  metal or plastic cup with handle
  aluminum tart pans
  wooden spools
  empty tape rolls
  small juice cans
  cardboard rolls cut up
  Non-toxic paint or Con-Tact paper

1. Punch holes in tart pans.
2. Remove ends of small cans, hammer down edges, and line with cloth tape.
3. Decorate spools, juice can, tape rolls, and cardboard rolls with paint or Con-Tact paper.
4. Thread string, shoe lace, or elastic through objects. Tie knots on both sides of tart pans.

These items should be able to spin when baby plays with them.

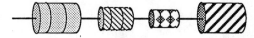

PEEK-A-BOO GAMES

• Glue a large picture of a baby onto a piece of cardboard. Tape pieces of fabric over body parts. Name parts of body for him as he lifts the fabric.
• With cloth tape, attach a piece of fabric to the top of an unbreakable mirror.
• Tape fabric over **Smiling Face Sheet** on page 22.

THE EXPLORER
9 to 14 Months

Dealing with your baby at this stage is a tremendous challenge. Trying to balance the need of your child to explore everything he sees and your desire for his safety and the preservation of your home is difficult and frustrating.

Your household will be much less stressful if you can take the time to "baby proof" your home so your child does not have to be confined by playpen or gates.

Since curiosity is the single most important quality that a child needs for learning, you don't want to squelch him with a thousand "no's" every day.

Your baby will spend most of his time on three different activities. The first is watching and learning about the mother, father or caretakers. The second is exploring the house and all the objects in it. The third is mastering his motor skills.

He will start speaking his first words at around 12 - 14 months. His method of moving around will change dramatically in this phase, from crawling to climbing, pulling to stand, "cruising" by holding on, and finally walking. Some very active 15-month-old babies will also learn to run and ride four wheeled toys.

Your child will also be developing progress in gross and fine motor skills while he works on manipulating small objects.

His preference of objects will be small, colorful, noisy and irregularly shaped ones. Hinged objects such as doors, lids on boxes, and cardboard books are very fascinating to him.

A collection of different small objects in a container will be sure to keep his interest as he takes them out and examines them. Objects around the house that show cause and effect such as light switches, flashlights, dimmer switches, and drain stoppers will be fun for him.

More elaborate peek-a-boo games such as hiding yourself behind a chair will be fun at this stage.

HINGED TOYS

Babies at this age love hinged objects.

Surprise Cupboard Door

2 4 x 6" pieces
of 1/2" plywood or masonite
4 x 6 piece of heavy fabric or
cloth tape
Wooden knob
Photo or picture
Clear Con-Tact paper

1. Sand wood until surface and edges are smooth.
2. Place one board on top of the other.
3. Glue fabric or tape to both boards on outside.
4. Glue knob to middle of one board on outside.
5. Glue a photo or a magazine picture to the inside of the
"cupboard." Cover with Con-Tact paper.

Change the picture every so often.

A whole series of **Custom Made Books** can be made from
inexpensive photo albums with self adhesive pages. For
simplicity, put only one picture on a page. Use pictures you
find in catalogs, magazines, greeting cards, and your own
photographs. Consider making the following books:

*   Photographs of relatives and friends
*   Pictures of familiar objects such a spoon, crib, chair
*   Pictures of animals
*   Pictures of food
*   Pictures of plants, trees, and flowers
*   Photographs of baby's favorite stuffed animals and toys
*   Pictures of clothes

A **Texture Book** can be made by removing plastic from the
pages of a photo album. Glue different textured fabrics and
materials (fur, rubber, satin, etc.) to cardboard. Try adding a
"squeaker" (available at hobby shops) under pieces of fabric.

STACKING AND NESTING TOYS

Some of the best stacking and nesting toys can be found in your kitchen. Pots and pans and plastic bowls are perfect toys for your baby to learn about increasing sizes and the mathematical concept of seriation, that is, this comes first, this comes second, and this comes third.

If you need to use your kitchen items for meal preparation you needn't look far to make baby's own stacking and nesting toys.

Milk Carton Stackers

Varied size milk cartons
Fabric, Con-Tact paper **or**
* wallpaper*
Glue

1. Cut off tops of cartons so bottoms are cube shaped.
2. Glue fabric, contact paper or wallpaper to outside.

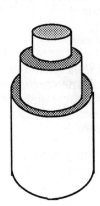

Tin Can Nesters

Tin cans of varying diameters
* and heights*
Fabric, Con-Tact paper **or**
* wallpaper*
Cloth tape

1. Remove one end of each can.
2. Pound down any sharp metal edges.
3. Cover rims with cloth tape.
4. Decorate the outside of the cans with fabric or contact paper.

Nesting Cups can be made from aerosol can caps of varying sizes.

Spindle Toy

Sturdy paper towel cardboard roll
Coffee can with plastic lid
Assorted colored plastic bracelets

1. Cut hole in lid with exacto knife or
scissors to match size of cardboard tube.
2. Pound down any sharp edges on coffee
can with hammer.
3. Insert tube into lid and place lid on can.
4. Provide plastic bracelets to stack on spindle.

Milk Carton Blocks

Milk cartons of varied size
Fabric, Con-Tact paper **or**
  wallpaper
Glue
Newspaper

1. Cut milk cartons cube shaped.
2. Stuff one carton with newspaper for stability.
3. Push container bottoms together to form cube.
4. Decorate outside of blocks with fabric, Con-Tact paper or
wallpaper.

BATH TIME TOYS

For simple bath time toys, collect 2 or 3 empty plastic bottles like those for shampoo, dishwashing liquid, or hand cream. Punch holes in the various bottles to make a **Bathtime Sprinkler** . These containers will be fun in the bath or outdoor wading pool. Show your baby how to work the bottles with spouts.

Other water play toys can include tea strainers, plastic funnels, plastic measuring cups and spoons, film canisters and colanders.

Washcloth Puppet

2 washcloths
Embroidery thread
Yarn

1. Cut out shape of head and arms on wash cloths.
2. Stitch together and leave an opening at bottom.
3. Embroider face on one or both sides.
4. Stitch pieces of yarn on head for hair.

Entertainment for the reluctant bather.

Floating Bath Toys

Sponges or corks
1 ft. light weight string

1. Poke holes in sponges or corks.
2. Thread string through the holes.
3. Tie the ends of the string together.
Point out to baby how the sponge changes when it gets wet.

Floating Shapes can be made by cutting geometric shapes, letters and numbers from styrofoam meat trays or dinner plates.

SAFETY NOTE

These toys should be used during supervised play. Make sure baby doesn't bite off pieces of cork, sponge, or styrofoam.

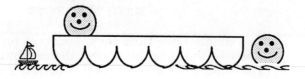

Boat and Crew

Styrofoam egg carton
Ping pong balls
Non-toxic paint
  (non water soluble)

1. Cut top off of egg carton.
2. Paint faces on ping pong balls.
Balls can float in the water or be placed in styrofoam "boat".

AROUND THE HOUSE

Make a collection of 30 or 40 objects. Find containers to put them in. Put about 5 - 10 items in each container and put container in different spots around the house where baby likes to play. (See list of household play objects at back of book.) These make quick items to grab when you want to entertain baby.

CHALLENGE
14 to 24 Months

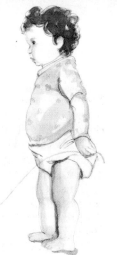

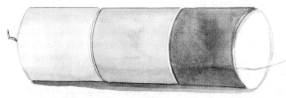

This period of your child's life is divided between exploring the world and a strong interest in the mother, father or caretaker. It is best for both of you to try and strike balance between these interests. Try to be available to your child, but also try to make your home interesting, so your child gets involved in independent playing for portions of the day.

Your toddler will also be mastering many motor skills such as walking, climbing, running, and jumping. Riding 4 wheeled vehicles challenges him.

In exploring the world he'll be examining qualities of objects and practicing simple skills such as dropping, throwing, opening, closing and swinging doors, and pouring water or sand. Operating switches and spinning wheels hold a great fascination for him.

Along with exploring the world and gaining control over his body, your child is also developing his sense of humor. He laughs at your antics and tries some of his own to make you laugh. He loves an audience. He loves the attention from being "cute." Your smiles are his reward.

But with the bonding that comes with this sense of humor, there is a negativeness which allows for autonomy. During this time it is best to strike a balance between letting your child have his way on occasion so he feels independent while continuing to set limits.

One of the great interests of children in this age group is water. Give him access to the sink, bathtub, dishpan, hose, or a kiddie pool. Add a couple of containers for channeling water and watch water become a favorite toy.

Another basic material is paper. Tissue paper, toilet paper, Kleenex, wax paper, magazines and junk mail are all potential toys. Cardboard and corrugated boxes, such as shoe boxes and gift boxes can hold your toddlers attention.

Books with stiff pages and recognizable illustrations fascinate this age group as will gymnastic equipment such as a small slide or a mini-jungle gym.

This age group also enjoys balls. A football, beach ball, tennis ball or ping pong ball all react differently when thrown. These balls also are a good way to involve parents or siblings in play with your toddler.

The following ideas may appeal to your child. If your toddler seems frustrated with any of them, put them away until he is a little older.

PULL TOY DESIGNS

Pull Car or Bus

Shoe box
Con-Tact paper
2 foot cord
People pictures

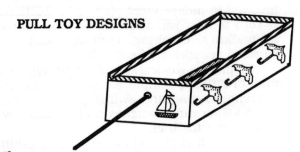

1. Punch a hole in the center of one end of the shoe box.
2. Slip 2 foot cord through hole and make knot on the inside of box.
3. Cover box with Con-Tact paper. Make windows with contrasting colored paper and paste pictures of family members in the windows. Cover windows with clear Con-Tact paper.

Pull trains can be made by tying a series of ice cream cartons or small boxes together.

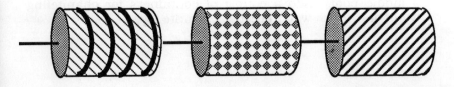

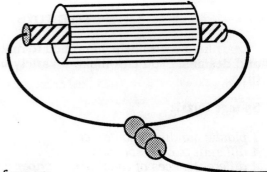

Musical Pull Toy

Paper towel tube
Orange juice can
Heavy string
Con-Tact paper
A few small bells

1. Remove both ends of orange
juice can and pound down sharp edges.
2. Cover can and paper towel tube with Con-Tact paper.
3. Slip paper towel tube inside orange juice can.
4. Slip heavy string through paper towel tube.
5. Thread bells on to string so they are inside tube.
6. Tie string together at about 12" from tubes. Continue to tie
a series of knots every 3".

Caterpillar Pull Toy

Orange juice can lids
Empty thread spools
Heavy weight string
Non-toxic paint
Jingle bell (optional)

1. Punch holes in juice can lids and hammer down any sharp
edges.
2. Alternate juice can lids and thread spools to make
caterpillar. Add a large bell at end for sound if desired.
3. Paint lids and spools caterpillar colors.

PUZZLE TOYS

Learning puzzles help your child to match up colors, shapes, and designs. You can make a variety of puzzles during this time.

Sponge Puzzle

1 plastic sandwich container
4 different colored sponges
4 different pieces of construction paper (same color as sponges)

1. Make a square 1/4 size of sandwich box.
2. Cut same size square from sponge and matching construction paper.
3. Paste paper squares to inside bottom of sandwich box.

Guide your child in placing the sponge squares on the color matched paper squares.

Pattern Puzzle

Wallpaper, wrapping paper, tin foil, or Con-Tact paper
Cardboard

1. With a pencil, divide one piece of cardboard into 4 squares.
2. Glue a different piece of paper to each section.
3. Cut a second piece of cardboard into 4 sections the same size as the squares on the board.
4. Cover each square with clear Con-Tact paper for durability.

Encourage baby to match squares to board.

Picture Puzzle

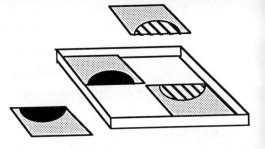

Colorful magazine picture
Cardboard
Clear Con-Tact paper
Shallow card board box
Large mailing envelope

1. Glue picture to cardboard and cut into 4 parts.
2. Cover with clear Con-Tact paper.
3. Draw outlines of puzzle shapes inside bottom of shallow box with heavy black pen.

   Don't stop with basic square puzzle. Exercise your creativity by making pie shaped, triangle shaped, or for the truly daring, paisley shaped puzzles.

Shape Sorter

   A shape sorter helps your child to learn size and proportion. First you will need to show him how to use the box. Later, he will show off his talents.

Empty box
Household objects
  ex: ping pong balls
       blocks
       coasters
       cookie cutters
Cloth tape
Con-Tact paper (optional)

1. Cut holes in the top of the box to match the size of the household objects.
2. Line holes with tape.
3. Cut hole in side of box for retrieval of objects.

You may want to "pretty-up" this toy by first covering the box with contact paper.

Certain toys can be made up teach your child about the world and develop his vocabulary.

Match Up

Plastic bowls or tumblers
Household objects
　ex:　ball
　　　key
　　　spool
　　　toothbrush
　　　comb

Tape or place pictures of objects in bowl or tumblers. Present your child with the corresponding object. Encourage him to match them up.

Feelie Box

Using an empty egg carton and some different textured fabrics, you can teach your toddler about rough, smooth, soft, furry, and other "feels."

Egg carton
Assorted fabrics
　ex:　tin foil
　　　sandpaper
　　　fake fur
　　　cotton ball
　　　terry cloth
　　　silky fabric
Glue

1. Cut small holes in domed side of egg carton.
2. Attach fabric to hole with glue.
3. Glue or tape carton.

Another toy that can be made with the same materials is a **Bean Bag Box.** Cut out 12 different shapes out of 2 x 3 inch assorted fabrics. Shapes can include hearts, squares, diamonds, or ovals. Fill shapes with dried beans, peas, or polyester filling. Place mini-bean bags in egg carton for your child to feel and transfer around. He can transfer bean bags from egg carton to muffin tin or ice cube tray.

Smell Box

The same egg carton idea can be varied to make a **Smell Experience Box** by using cotton balls soaked in different substances such as vanilla or almond extract, perfume, onion juice, etc. Talk about these different odors with your child. "This is sour. This is sweet."

Variation of Smell Box

Scented cotton balls can be placed inside empty herb or spice jars with perforated lids.

RAINY DAY RECIPES

These are recipes you can make up ahead of time and have stored in your refrigerator.

Play Dough

1 cup flour
1/2 cup salt
1 tablespoon oil
2 teaspoons Cream of Tartar
1 cup of water
A few drops of food coloring

1. Combine ingredients in a pot.
2. Stir over low heat until thick.
3. Form into a ball and store in a covered container.

Edible Finger Paint

1 envelope unflavored or flavored gelatin
1 cup cold water
1/2 cup cornstarch
2 cups boiling water

1. Add 1/4 cup cold water to gelatin and set aside.
2. Mix 3/4 cup cold water with cornstarch in sauce pan and stir until smooth.
3. Slowly stir boiling water into cornstarch mixture.
4. Cook over medium heat. Stir mixture constantly until it boils and is clear. Remove from heat and stir in gelatin mixture.
5. Divide mixture into jars. Color with food coloring, fruit drink powder, soy sauce or grape juice.

You can add flavors like vanilla, peppermint, lemon, or almond extract. Keep paint in refrigerator several days before using.

Edible Paste

1/4 cup boiling water
1/2 cup flour

1. Add flour into boiling water.
2. Stir over low heat until shining and thick.

Store in plastic container in refrigerator

Soap Crayons

1/8 cup water
7/8 cup Ivory Soap Flakes
Food coloring
Ice cube tray or popsicle molds

1. Mix water and soap flakes together to form a thick paste.
2. Add food coloring, and stir until thoroughly mixed (to color of your liking).
3. Spoon into ice cube trays or popsicle molds.
4. Dry in warm place 1 — 2 days until soap paste is hard.

Now your child can decorate the bathtub or himself to his heart's content.

Bubbles

1 cup liquid dishwashing detergent (Joy or Dawn work best)
2 cups warm water
3 tablespoons glycerine (purchased at drug store)
1/2 teaspoon sugar

Mix together and store in an airtight container.

MAKING BUBBLES

Once you have made the above recipe, there are dozens of ways you can help your child make bubbles.

Fill a cake pan with about 1/2" of Bubble solution. Take a strawberry basket, a colander, or a plastic six pack holder. Dunk it in the solution, then wave it through the air and let the bubbles fly.

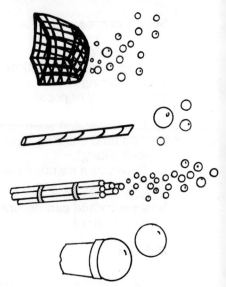

You can teach your child to blow bubbles with a plastic funnel or a plastic straw cut on the slant.

Several plastic straws taped together can be used to help your child blow hundreds of little bubbles.

A styrofoam cup with a hole poked in the bottom can be used for your child to make big bubbles.

WATER , SAND AND DIRT TOYS

Many of your child's bath time toys easily can be used for sand and dirt toys. He will love scooping up dirt or sand and transferring it to different containers. Funnels and colanders make water and sand take on different properties.

You can make a sandbox out of an old truck tire or kiddie pool. If your sand box is outdoors its a good idea to cover it when not in use to keep the sand dry and discourage the neighborhood cats from using it.

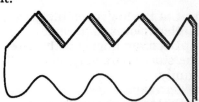

Sand Combs

*4" x 8" heavy cardboard
or thin wood sanded smooth*

1. Draw pattern on 8" side of cardboard or wood.
2. Cut out pattern with exacto knife or saw.
3. Smooth edges with sandpaper.

Make **Scoopers** out of large bleach containers by cutting off the sides at an angle. Sand any rough edges until smooth.

THEATRICS

Finger Puppets

These make story time or song time more fun.

Old gloves
Pens
Material Scraps

1. Cut the fingers off the gloves.
2. Hem gloves to prevent unraveling
3. Decorate fingers with material or non-toxic pens to look like story characters, like the Three Pigs, or members of the family.

Variation on Finger Puppets

Leave gloves intact and create a family of characters per glove to match stories.

Felt Boards

This is another way to make story or song time fun.

Assorted colored felt
Cardboard

1. Cover cardboard with large piece of felt.
2. Make objects such as trees and characters such as the Wolf in Red Riding Hood.

Kiddie Band

Earlier in the book I've described how to make a **Drum** and Shaker **Rattles** for baby. Use these to make or accompany music.

Kazoo

This is another instrument for your child to play along with.

Cardboard tube
Wax paper or aluminum foil
Rubber band

1. Cut a piece of wax paper or foil a few inches larger than the tube opening.
2. Use rubber band to hold wax paper or foil in place.
3. Punch hole one inch from covered end.
4. Teach your child to hum or sing "doo-doodle-doo" in open end of tube.

PLAY HOUSE

Toyhouse

Make houses for his toys and garages for his cars out of cardboard boxes. Draw windows and decorate house with crayons. Make doors by using cloth tape as a hinge.

Mail box

Let your child stuff your junk mail into a mail box made from an oatmeal box. Put a hole large enough to accommodate the junk. Line the hole and the rim of box with cloth tape.

Let your child stuff his mail box, then empty it out and start all over again. This can be a very absorbing activity.

Table House

Make a play house for your child by putting a sheet over a card table or dining room table. Be sure to leave one side open. Your child won't mind playing in his "house" as long as he can see out.

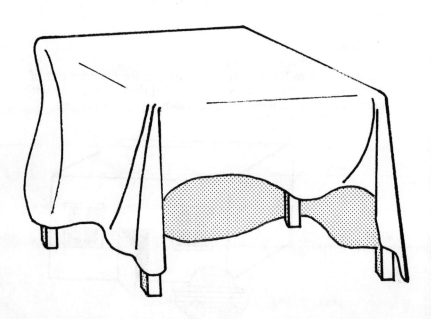

Toy Storage Unit

Now that you've constructed all these wonderful toys, where do you put them all? Here is an idea to keep the toys organized and visible.

15 Cylindrical ice cream containers
(collect during summer months from ice creameries)
Colored Con-Tact paper
String

1. Cover ice cream cartons with contact paper.
2. Arrange cartons in pyramid shape. (see illustration)
3. Punch holes in cartons where they meet and tie with string to hold together. (If necessary secure with cloth tape at back.)

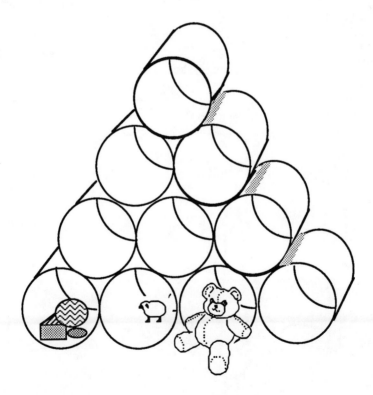

HOUSEHOLD OBJECTS AS TOYS

Throughout this book, household objects have been used as "toys." Play is important to your child. It is not only a means of entertainment, but a means of mastering skills and making connections. Your child may be more interested in your pots and pans than his plastic ducks because the pots make more noise and the lids fit. This is learning.

Here is a list of household toys. I'm sure as you search your drawers and cupboards, you or your child will find more.

It is important to check these household toys for safety. Make sure there are no sharp edges or splinters.

- Pots and pans with fitted lids
- Sets of measuring cups and spoons
- Empty milk cartons
- Oatmeal boxes
- Plastic jars and lids
- Junk mail
- Plastic dishes, cups, and coasters
- Empty spools of thread
- Cardboard tubes (toilet paper and paper towel)
- Margarine tubs
- Wooden spoons
- Plastic cookie cutters
- Popsicle mold
- Meat baster
- Funnels
- Strainers
- Rubber spatula
- Bottle stopper
- Colander
- Pastry brush
- Plastic ice cube tray
- Unbreakable mirror
- Plastic lazy susan
- Flashlight
- Napkin rings
- Vacuum cleaner attachments
- Fingernail brush
- Shoe horn
- Bird call whistle
- Cassette tape box
- Key ring
- Band Aid box with hinged lid
- Film cans
- Cardboard boxes
- Playing cards

Also Available from Bear Creek Publications:

The authors provide parent-tested tips for:
- Trave! Planning
- Coping with Hotels & Motels
- Restaurant Survival
- Airplane Travel
- Car Travel
- Train Travel
- Coping with Illness and Allergies
- Traveling with Several Children
- Equipment --What you need and what you can do without.

$5.95•80 Pages•Perfect Bound

To receive your copy of *Take Your Baby and Go!*, complete the order form on the next page.

You may order additional copies of **No Bored Babies** direct from the publisher. It makes a great gift for friends, new or expectant parents.

Please send me:
____ copies of NO BORED BABIES at $4.95 ea.
____ copies of TAKE YOUR BABY AND GO! at $5.95 ea.

Name _____

Address _____

City _____ **State** _____ **Zip** _____

Sales Tax: Please add 8.2% for books shipped to Washington addresses.

Shipping: Add $1.50 for first book and 50 cents for each additional book.

Payment:
____ Check
____ Credit Card ___ Visa ___ MasterCard
Card Number: _____
Name on Card: _____
Exp. date: _____/_____

Send payment to:
BEAR CREEK PUBLICATIONS
2507 Minor Avenue East
Seattle, WA 98102
(206) 322-7604

Telephone Orders: Call Toll Free 1-800-326-6566. Have your Visa or MasterCard ready.

Discounts available for larger orders. Call or write for details.